Whose Crazy Idea Was That?

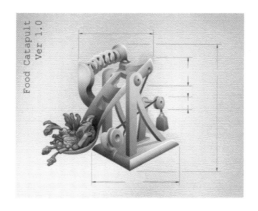

Food Catapult
Ver 1.0

Claire Craig

sundance

A Haights Cross Communications Company

Published by
Sundance Publishing
P.O. Box 740
One Beeman Road
Northborough, MA 01532–0740
800-343-8204
www.sundancepub.com

First published 2002 by
Blake Education, Locked Bag 2022, Glebe 2037, Australia
Exclusive United States Distribution: Sundance Publishing

Design by Cliff Watt in association with
Sundance Publishing

Whose Crazy Idea Was That?
ISBN 0-7608-6693-7

Photo Credits
p. 7 (bottom) Absolutely Mad Inventions, A.E. Brown and H.A. Jeffcott, Dover
Publications; p. 10-11 photolibrary.com; p. 15 Made in Mexico Hula Hoop ® is
a designated trademark of ©2002 Wham-O, Inc. All Rights Reserved.;
p. 16 photolibrary.com; p. 17 (top) Top Hat Entertainment;
p. 19 AAP Image; p. 24-25 photolibrary.com; p. 26 photolibrary.com;
p. 27–29 photolibrary.com.

Printed in Canada

Table
of Contents

The Wacky World of Inventions

**There's no doubt about it.
Some people have crazy ideas
for inventions.**

Is it your job to clear the table of dirty
dishes after dinner? Then you need a
"dishwashing dinner table." There's no
need to clear away the mess—just flip the
table over and wash the dishes right there.

Believe it or not, someone really did come
up with this mad invention! And there are
many more ideas just as crazy as this one.

Back to the Drawing Board

Most inventors apply for a **patent** when they think they have a good idea. A patent is a legal document that proves who owns an invention. It stops other people from stealing an idea for 20 years. After that, anyone can use the idea! But the idea is only the beginning. Some ideas look good on paper . . . and that's just where they stay. Would you want to use these three ideas that didn't make it?

Idea 1

Have you lost a lot of food fights lately?
You need a machine to propel food into a crowd.

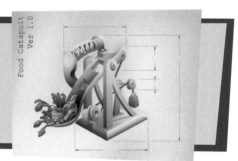

Idea 2

Wondering what to do with a dead relative?
Put them inside a large glass block. If the block is too big for your room, you can use a smaller glass block for the head.

Idea 3

Do you have problems getting up in the morning? What about:

- a bed that automatically ejects you when the alarm goes off?
- an alarm that pours water on you?
- an alarm that hits you?

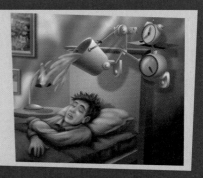

An Alarm Clock That Strikes . . . You!

To apply for a patent, an inventor must draw a diagram and write a description of his or her invention. Not all patents are granted, so the inventor has to give plenty of information to convince the **Patent Office** that the invention is new and useful.

Every patent has a number.

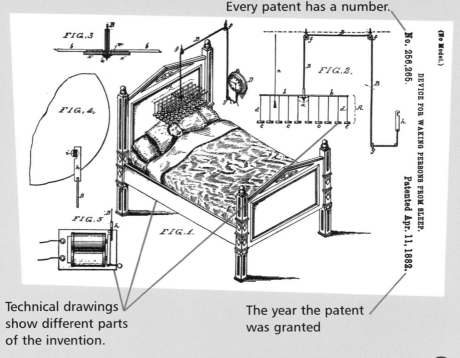

Technical drawings show different parts of the invention.

The year the patent was granted

Ahead of Their Time

Sometimes ideas for inventions sound crazy because they are ahead of their time. The first fax machine, which was invented and used way back in 1865, is one example.

Giovanni Caselli, a tutor living in Siena, Italy, invented a large, heavy machine called a pantelegraph. It could send and receive

CASELLI'S pantelegraph was about 2 meters (6.5 ft) tall.

How Does It Work?

1 A message is written with ink on a metal plate.

2 The plate is placed under a pendulum.

3 The pendulum's metal tip swings over the plate, touching the surface.

4 When the tip touches an uninked section, it causes an **electrical circuit** to be completed.

an actual copy of written notes or pictures. His neighbors called him crazy. Some people thought he was using an evil form of magic. The French government did use the machine for a few years, but then it disappeared. Maybe it cost too much money. Or maybe it was just a good idea ahead of its time. Today fax machines are used all over the world.

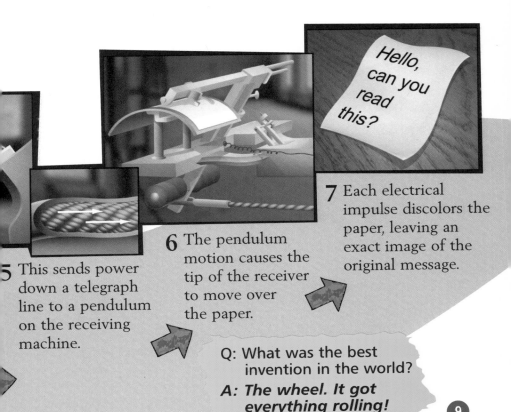

5 This sends power down a telegraph line to a pendulum on the receiving machine.

6 The pendulum motion causes the tip of the receiver to move over the paper.

7 Each electrical impulse discolors the paper, leaving an exact image of the original message.

Q: What was the best invention in the world?

A: *The wheel. It got everything rolling!*

Bright Lights

I've just invented an inventor!

There's no limit on how many patents one person can hold. One very busy inventor was Thomas Edison. With his team of workers, he invented the electric lightbulb, the **phonograph**, which later played records, and movie cameras. In all, he took out 1,093 patents!

Edison also liked a good joke. He was very famous, and everything he did and said was news. He liked to give reporters interesting things to write about. Legend has it that in 1920 he told a reporter he was working on a machine that could talk to the dead. Many newspapers reported the story. Years later, Edison admitted he had made it up!

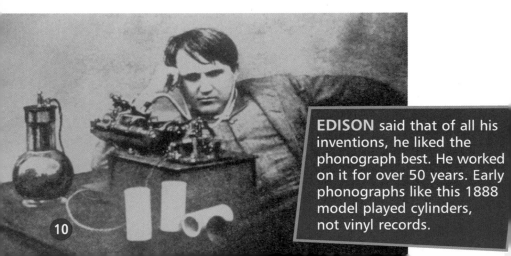

EDISON said that of all his inventions, he liked the phonograph best. He worked on it for over 50 years. Early phonographs like this 1888 model played cylinders, not vinyl records.

THE ROOF of Edison's motion picture-making studio could be opened, and the whole building rotated to get the best sunlight.

WHEN HE INVENTED the lightbulb, Edison filled approximately 40,000 notebook pages with drawings and notes.

More Everyday Inventions

YEAR	INVENTION	INVENTOR	COUNTRY
3000 B.C.	marbles	unknown inventor	Egypt
100	comics	unknown inventor	Rome
200	wheelbarrow	Chuko Liang	China
1281	eyeglasses	Silvano Armato	Italy
1642	calculator	Blaise Pascal	France
1762	sandwich	the Earl of Sandwich	England
1770	roller skates	Joseph Merlin	Belgium
1770	toothbrush	William Addis	England
1855	refrigerator	Jacob Perkins	England
1901	vacuum cleaner	H. Cecil Booth	England
1903	windshield wiper	Mary Anderson	United States
1957	Liquid Paper®	Bette Nesmith Graham	United States
1978	bionic ear	Graeme Clark	Australia

How Did They Think of That?

It's gooey like rubber. It bounces and it stretches. Play with it, or use it to take dog hair off the furniture. It's Silly Putty.

Though the name suggests that it was invented for fun, that was not what happened. Silly Putty was the stuff left over after engineers worked with other materials. No one knew what to do with it. Then someone realized you could have a lot of fun with it!

Some inventions are like that. Someone thinks of a new way to use something that has been around for a long time.

Hooping It Up

As long ago as 1000 B.C., Greek and Roman children played with hoops made from vines. In colonial days in America, children rolled barrel  hoops along the streets, guiding them with sticks. Australian children used bamboo hoops in gym classes at school. But in 1958, the idea was taken one step further. That was the year the Hula Hoop, a hollow plastic hoop, appeared in stores.

This toy became a huge success. People held contests to see who could twirl the most hoops around their waists, arms, wrists, legs, feet—even around their heads and necks. But the company that made them was unable to get a patent for such an ancient idea. So soon others were making toys like Spin-a-Hoops and Hoop-d-dos. It is estimated that between 60 and 100 million hoops were sold in two years!

UFPT
Unidentified Flying
Pie Tin

HULA HOOPS were made in all colors and patterns. At the peak of the craze, one company manufactured 20,000 a day.

Invasion of the Frisbees

In the 1950s, people were talking about flying saucers. Some people thought that green aliens would soon invade Earth! Walter Frederick was caught up in the craze. He invented a toy disc that glided through the air and looked like a flying saucer. But he didn't know what to call it. Then he learned about students at Yale University. In the 1870s, their favorite piemaker was a man named William Frisbie. They would eat his pies, then play games throwing the empty pie tins. Walter had discovered the name for his new toy. The Frisbee was here!

From Nature to Velcro

Some inventions seem to mirror things in the natural world. When George de Mestral, a Swiss engineer, went for a walk in 1948, he had a close encounter with a prickly burdock plant. After brushing against the plant, he realized that his clothes were covered with spiny **burrs**. As he removed the clinging burrs, he saw that they were covered with hundreds of small hooks. Then, he had an idea. . . .

After seven years of experimenting, he finally succeeded in making two nylon strips. One strip had lots of tiny loops and the other had tiny hooks. When the strips were pressed together, they stuck firmly. Today, Velcro has many practical uses—and a few crazy ones like Velcro wall jumping!

BURR under the microscope

VELCRO under the microscope

How to Velcro Wall Jump

1. Make sure your suit is made with the Velcro side opposite to that on the wall!
2. Jump off the trampoline and hit the wall so you stick to it.
3. Now try to move about—without falling off.

Hint! For a softer landing when it's time to get unstuck, roll yourself slowly down the wall.

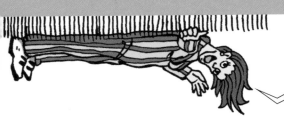

Help!

VELCRO wall jumping

Other Natural Similarities

Nature	Invention
dandelion seed floating to the ground	parachute
birds and flying fish	airplane
wasps building nests from chewed wood	making paper
protective plates of bone on armadillo	armor
rose thorns	barbed wire
camouflage used by animals and insects	camouflage in war
centipedes with jointed sections	trains
beaver	dam building
whale baleen for filtering krill	sieves, fishing nets
rattlesnake's rattle	alarms

When One Thing Leads to Another

Sometimes an idea that doesn't work can lead to an idea that does. Levi Strauss didn't set out to invent blue jeans, but that's what happened.

Strauss went to San Francisco in 1853 when the California Gold Rush was in full swing. He hoped to sell canvas to the **prospectors** so they could use this thick, sturdy material to make tents and wagon covers. But he made a mistake. Nobody wanted to buy his canvas.

What the prospectors really needed were pants. People worked hard in the gold fields, and their pants wore out quickly! So Levi Strauss made pants out of the brown canvas he couldn't sell. They quickly sold out. Then Strauss switched to a heavy blue fabric. Today, Levi's blue jeans are worn in every country in the world.

Sure could use a sturdy pair of pants!

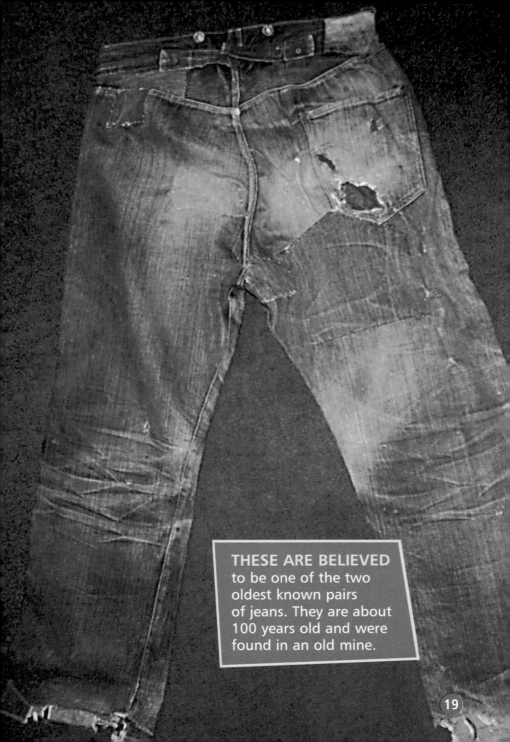

THESE ARE BELIEVED to be one of the two oldest known pairs of jeans. They are about 100 years old and were found in an old mine.

19

Pop! Goes the Invention

Accidents happen . . . and they can lead to great ideas. Sometimes those ideas can stare you in the face—or send a message to your stomach. Other times it can be years before you realize you've invented something pretty good.

I've invented the doughnut!

In 1905, 11-year-old Frank Epperson mixed some flavored powder with water. By mistake, he left the drink outside all night—with the stirring stick still in it. It was a very cold night. In the morning, Frank saw that the drink had frozen to the stick. It tasted delicious!

Eighteen years later, Frank remembered the frozen sticks. He applied for a patent and began to produce Epsicles. By now he had children of his own, and they didn't like the name. They changed it to Popsicles.

Chips to Order!

In 1853, George Crum was working in a restaurant kitchen in Saratoga Springs, New York. George was grumpy because he had a customer who kept sending back his fried potatoes saying he wanted them to be thinner and fried longer! So George sliced the potatoes as thin as thin could be. Then he fried them until their sides curled. George thought that would keep the man quiet. But the customer loved the potato chips! And so do we.

Ha ha ha! This will fix him!

Getting an Idea Off the Ground

The crowd was quiet. The wings felt strong on his back. He ran toward the edge of the cliff. Faster and faster with his arms flapping . . .

Daredevil or crazy? Who were these people trying to fly like birds? Many ideas for getting off the ground turned into falling flops. It took hundreds of years before people actually made it into the air.

An Ideas Man

I'll get you one day!

Leonardo da Vinci was a **genius**. He was a painter, a **scholar**, and a scientist who lived in the 1400s. But his ideas were far ahead of the times in which he lived. He drew designs for amazing things people thought were impossible: bicycles, parachutes, and the craziest of all—flying machines.

Leonardo believed that people would be able to fly in machines. He studied everything he could about birds. He drew plans for flapping wings attached to a person. He even designed a helicopter.

Leonardo da Vinci was able to imagine what might be invented in the future. Who knows what fantastic ideas he might come up with if he were alive today!

AN AGING Leonardo da Vinci (1452–1519) at work

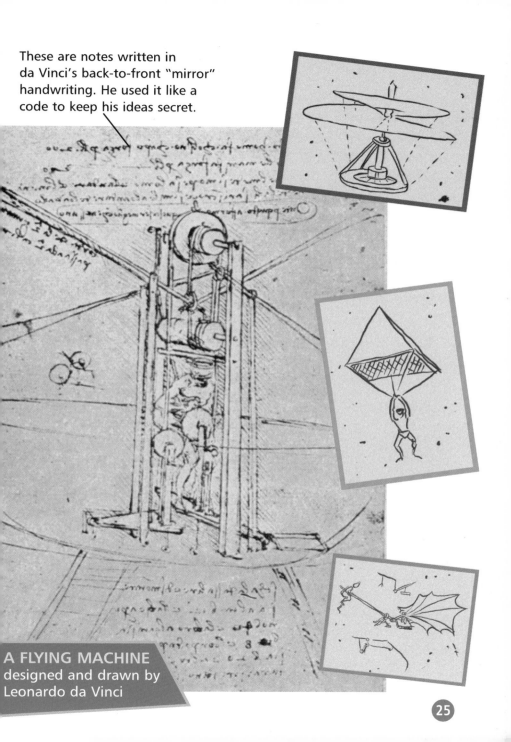

These are notes written in da Vinci's back-to-front "mirror" handwriting. He used it like a code to keep his ideas secret.

A FLYING MACHINE designed and drawn by Leonardo da Vinci

Flying High

In 1782, two Frenchmen, Joseph and Etienne Montgolfier, made a balloon out of paper and cloth. Then they lit a fire beneath the balloon. The hot air rising from the fire pushed the balloon up into the sky. The Montgolfier brothers decided that the balloon was now ready for passengers. They must have been short on human **volunteers** because the first passengers were a sheep, a duck, and a rooster!

A SHEEP, a duck, and a rooster swing in a cage beneath the balloon. The aim was to see if living creatures could survive such a flight. They did!

In 1793, two other Frenchmen stepped forward and said they would take to the skies in a Montgolfier balloon. They stayed in the air for 25 minutes and traveled more than 8 kilometers (5 miles). This balloon was the first successful flying craft to carry humans. Now anything seemed possible!

Other Early Attempts to Fly

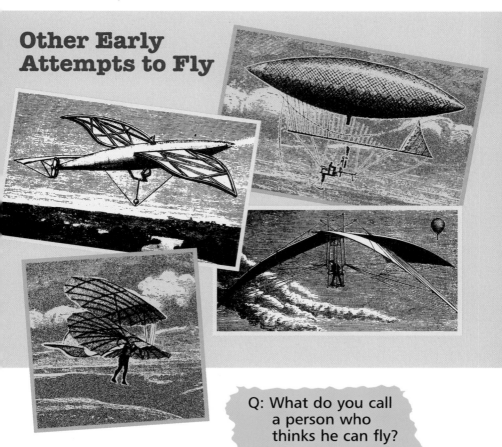

Q: What do you call a person who thinks he can fly?

A: **Plane crazy**

The Wright Stuff

Orville and Wilbur Wright wanted to fly. While they were at school, they read all about the theories of flight and built kites to learn how they flew. They studied **gliders**, which had been invented in 1804, and wondered how they could improve them.

They designed their own glider and added a 12-**horsepower** gasoline engine to it. They called it *The Flyer.* In 1903, they tossed a coin on Kill Devil Hill in North Carolina to see who would fly the plane. Orville Wright won the toss and became the pilot of the first powered flight in history.

Orville

Wilbur

Orville lying on the lower wing

We have liftoff!

Wilbur

WRIGHT BROTHERS' first powered flight in 1903, just as the aircraft left the ground. The flight lasted for about 12 seconds.

Soon aircraft became better and faster, and aviators flew around the world. Suddenly, the world seemed much smaller. People wondered where they could fly to next. Maybe to the moon?

Another crazy idea that came true!

Fact File

The first submarine was invented in 1620. It was basically two rowboats with a skin-tight covering. It could stay underwater for three hours.

In the late 19th century, false teeth were made out of celluloid, a very early ki of plastic. Unfortunately, h things, like a cup of tea, m the celluloid melt!

I need another set of arms!

It's thought that the larges hearing aid ever invented was a throne! People spoke into its hollow arms and the sound traveled into tubes in the ears of King John of Portugal.

Arms for eyeglasses were invented 400 years after the glasses themselves. Until then, people had to balance their glasses on their nose.

SUPER 02

What mess.

The first vacuum cleaner invented was as big as a refrigerator. It took two people to operate. One had to push it while the other pointed the hose.

GLOSSARY

burrs the rough, prickly cases around the seeds of some plants

electrical circuit the path through which electricity flows

genius someone who has very high mental ability and creative, original ideas

gliders motorless airplanes that glide from one point to another using gravity or air currents

horsepower a unit of measurement of power

patent a government grant to an inventor, giving him or her the right to be the only one to make, use, and sell an invention for a set period of time

Patent Office the government department that grants patents

phonograph "talking machine"—the early name for record players, which were in use before CD players

prospectors people who search for gold and other minerals

scholar a person of great learning

volunteers people who offer to do something for someone else

INDEX